Bad Queen Behavior

Meg Valentino

Presentation by *BookLeaf Publishing*

Web: www.bookleafpub.com

E-mail: info@bookleafpub.com

ISBN: 9789395087216

First edition 2022

DEDICATION

For Liz.

Find the one with your name.

ACKNOWLEDGEMENT

To all the women woven into my life, short
threads or a permanent sweater, thank you.
Thank you for your honesty, loving me, loving
yourself, and moving to live emboldened in your
bad queen behavior.

My mother, my sisters, Alyse and Lauryn, Id
never have accomplished even one written word
without you. Alyse, your determination, your
boldness in who you are as a person, and the
love you have for your people keeps me going,
keeps me breathing, and holds me up when I
fall. Lauryn, my kid sister, your free loving spirit
carries me in the moments I feel the smallest, I
know you will always be just around the corner
for me and the girls. I love you both.

Thank you to my Ma, one of the strongest
women I know, in spirit and body. Thank you for
molding me into the woman I have become and
am still finding.
To my aunties, Amy and Tina for being the
guidance and stronghold in my life ll never take
for granted. And my Mamma, you can't ever
leave us, we love you and need you to much!

Bad Queen
Behavior

They tell us how to live.
This one chance we have been handed
silent at the womb
One, Two, Three

Scream.

Repeat.

Repeat when adolescent innocence shakes free,
Ready to cloak anothers youth until something
all too real
shakes it loose again.
Unclasped by body and man.

One. Two. Three.

Scream.

Look in the glass,
joy and imagination have lost its way.
Something

someone
took it from you.
Lifted from your back pocket.
Blue jeans forced to the ground.
Prying out a slice of your soul.
The glass looks back.

One… Two… Three…

SCREAM.

Dont tell.

Isn't that the problem,
no one told us what becoming a grown up would
be like.
The broken and sad parts smile in their teeth.
Was it a secret on purpose?
Were they silenced by the internal shrieks?
Worn in lines to keep from exhausted lips.
No one can want this.

Tell the looking glass it can have someone else.
This isnt the life screamed for at birth.

Tossed away.
Still nude.
Still helpless.
Still leaking fools' tears.

Still

One.

Two.

Three.

Scream.

Break the glass. Clean the blood. Look at your
hands, a clean slate.

Be the bad they told you not to be.
Live like the Queen banned books planted in
your dreams.
Embrace the behavior they told you wasnt
properly lady like.
One… Two… Three…

Bad. Queen. Behavior.

Her, Closer

Look closer.
Is she happy?
Does it matter?
Look closer.

Vagabond or fool? Does it matter?
Look closer.

Diamond or stone. Does it matter?
Look closer.

Pick up your mind. Is it heavy?
Light as a feather stiff as a board.
Does it matter?

Look closer. Is she her own?

She said.
He said.
He said.

She never said.

Will it matter?
Look closer.

She's a Monster

Conviction in a gone mental fog.
I'd let it loose
but it doesn't want to leave.
Its residence is invisible to you,
not to me.
A monster distorts my thoughts all day.
Sometimes it leaves,
but it never can stay away.

Hide then Deceive

A sour pit grows in my stomach, rising to my
heart, invading my thoughts.
I know this stranger.

It always finds me in the corners, attempting to
play the hiding game under a scared heart. Its
perfume clothed in my assaults.

I did this; I put myself here.
No blame but my own.
No one else to cast hooded eyes on, no red eyes
in the dead of night to hate, to fear, only silent
anger and pain bellowing through anguished
eyes.

Sometimes, if I delude myself enough,
I can ignore its presence.
Pretend I am rid of it, that it doesn't make any
difference.

That I can slip out of my hiding place with ease,
dropping my atrocities, my monsters planted at
the end of starless fingertips extending in the
dark.

Haven't you had enough? I cry to myself.
Don't you have a soul? I shriek into the
obsidian.

I shower my character with repercussions
provided by teetering thoughts of life.
I hastily let the truth flood over me, let it
evaporate, sinking back into my skin where it
can continue to leach the life, the happiness out
of my others.

Wasn't I supposed to love them the most?

But how, then, I ask my closed eyes, do I love
myself?
Weren't you supposed to figure it all out?
Each love
each person
the versions of yourself?

My only capable answer, pitiful in its
unbraiding, is the last gasp of
 air sucked into the lion's mouth
at the second it deceives itself.

Crooked Thoughts

Have you ever felt as if you are drowning in the
stillness?
The insipid fluidity of the same,
the same,
the same.

You can flip one day over the next
without distorting its image.
Shrieking and withering on the inside.
Plain and unremarkable on the outside.

It's a cool feeling, a slithering thing
woven into your fingers
your eyes
your feet.

Thoughts rapping crooked insinuations of
identity,
disturbing the quiet places,
hostile in your mind.
An echo in its pressure confuses the glass,
settling the perception of a thousand minds.

Once silent voices claim purchase

of their reservations,
reciting stories pleaded not to be told;
There isn't Enough
There isn't Anything
There isn't You
each tale ends the same.

Alone in the duplicitous spreading
of unremarkable skin
shivering like a sheet tossed over the dead,
its chilling kindliness inscribing;
no one will bother to find you here.

Spare moments too greedy to swallow,
for a turn of the eye long enough to see
what still lingers of me.

Carousel

Really, we are all blundering along on a
carousel,
bodies run down and weathered
mechanical horses plastered with permanently
false eyes
bobbing up and down to the same tune.

A procession of Stepford wives never coloring
outside the lines.

How mindless it must be
to be a fastened fool for society,
glued to an untruth.
Round and round they go on that carousel of
lies.
Built to wrangle a formation,
a follow the leader.
Round and round
they go.
Round and
round.

Stop.

Now,
go.

Take me Apart

Mind aghast
Face not a mask
Eye on the glass
Who is the ugliest
Till the last.

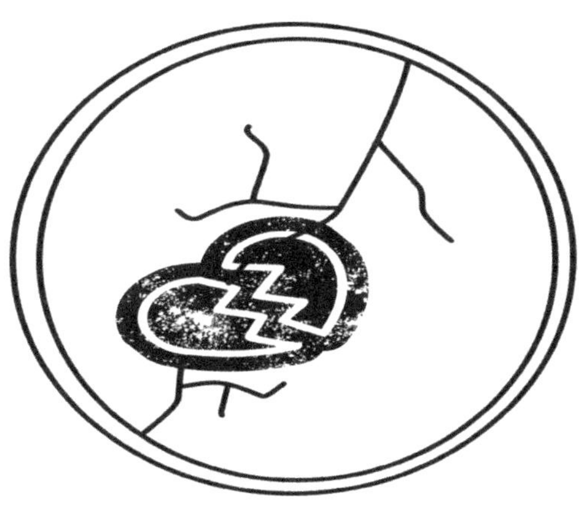

There, Hiding

There is a rattling at the door.
Which door, I am not sure.
There, the drop of a foot, then its mate,
smacking its heel on the world it strides.
Where the feet intend to go
and who they drag with them
I do not know.

What burns beneath the surface,
hiding
not hiding,
ignites all the same.

Would it be gripped if provoked?
Heat whelms coveted air.
A profound breath doesn't always obstruct
death.
To take hold of the flame
…well
that,
that would free the pain.

Hand in the Venom

Lies, covered truths.
I ventured into dark places
in search of a nameless thing
that laid a poison on me.

Don't blame the venom.
Hand of fate flexed its bones
accepting with consent.

I couldn't find my way
as a mother,
as a wife,
as a person.

I scattered in unlike directions,
latching on to the dregs of living, forgetting, or
choosing
to destroy the people I said I loved
to serve the wretched cravings inside of me.

Horrid

I fell to wits end, vowed
I would not self-sabotage,
I would end the repetitions of
feeding and throttling my glaring self-hatred.

I stoked the fire and fed it poison anyway.

I neglected deadlines, due dates, children,
hunger.
I felt no burden.
I did not feel as if much mattered.

I argued with panicked thoughts
roused by ghostly hands none other than mine.
I struggled with them, called them hideous
things.
All the while looking at my reflection with a
sick awareness.

A genocidal hunger melted resilience already
lost
I thought to myself,
that the solitary ache fixated over my bones…

that's what makes the living do horrid things.

Illuminations End

I sit at my desk, in my blue velvet chair, its corners well known, shaped just for me. Everything is slightly worn, chipped curves and split wood. There is a settled feeling that radiates what home feels like, its comforts and open arms. The kind of place you can sink into and smile.

I sit at my desk without commitments or deadlines, not in favor of a passionate tale to write or something intoxicating to read, not even to find my breath again; discover ease in my weary limbs.

I sit at my desk looking out the picture window; its panes reflect warm shifts of light, soft, and buttery illuminations.

I sit at my desk searching the glass, wringing my hands together in an anxious gesture, waiting to see what I long for the most—lying in wait for a hopeful impossibility to appear, green eyes hunting it down in feverish heartbeats.

I beg the window with its perfectly fitted corners; its creamy white trim to encase my reveries parading in circles in the spaces where time stops and lazy dreaming takes over, turning grand thoughts into something that aches instead of beams.

I sit at my desk, growing impatient, impeding judgments of anger washing over my prudently put together milky golden landscape.

I despise anger, a useless emotion. It drips into my blood, snaking its way close to my heart, dancing at its edges, raging the siren of war. It rushes and flips over inside of itself, a growing thing that bids to give me new skin.

I sit at my desk, the gleam of the glass giving way to the shadows of nightfall. One lone street lamp sputters on its electricity before it originates to life. I see its small flicker of light, its tiny obscurities casting a ghastly glare over the pavement.

It sparks on while the moon wakes.
I break into puddles of ignorant daylight that thought it would keep shining into the night.

I sit at my desk; I see nothing. I do not see twin beams of a car's headlights leading its procession up the road, turning its glower onto

my driveway, slicking itself over the red paint on
the wooden siding.

I do not hear the harsh metal of a door spit open
and slam shut. My heart does not race at the
sound of thick footsteps, sure-footed on their
path. I see no glimpse of him rounding the
corner, the window catching his familiar figure.

There is no serendipitous moment where eyes
catch one another at the same second; there is no
shiver of excitement passed between one gaze to
another.
The glass does not reflect his lengthy body
stepping up to the door, twisting the knob,
finding it free of its lock, free to push open, and
come inside.

I sit at my desk; the blackness only just lit with
the smallest piece of synthetic electricity, the
stars in the black sky holding up illuminations
end.

I sit at my desk, looking out the window, finding
myself looking back, not the face I have greedily
conjured from fond memories into existence.

I investigate the glass, forcing myself to study
my reflection, examine its distorted places

softened by the small lamp at my side, echoing
the same small effort as its twin, failing the
darkness in the street.

I look at myself and try to see the things that live
delicately inside of me, past the daydreams and
false realities, past the bodily desires and the
aches of missing. I don't blink, my eyes draining
of their impending tears, a burning building at
their base.

I sit at my desk, forcing my voice to tell my
reflection in a shaky, whisper of a declaration,
not losing eye contact with the picture-perfect
window that wanted something lovelier to
reflect, that he is not coming back.

Not at nightfall, not at mornings sunrise, not in
the versions of worlds spun with precision.

The place reserved in my mind for hopeful
recitations now settles a nightmarish shadow.
One that speaks in grim accusations, drenched in
a raven call for nevermore, obsidian eyes
speaking to me-

No more.

The Menace

Don't wipe the stars from my eyes.
What do you expect when the mind is a menace
and the heart doesn't beat.
Time falls away with the stillness of a summer
morning
like the sharp edges of a rusted knife
waiting to cut deep into the ripples of time
at just the right moment
when it will trouble the most.

Beverly Hills

How can I sit here, tears spilling through
makeup,
heart squeezing itself to impalement,
while Beverly Hills sprawls before me
money glistening on four wheels
Rodeo Drive grand around its palm trees,
and still, cry.

They burn and run their games on a Beverly
Hills balcony.
Leering into the sun, tell me to stop.
Stop feeling it all in a thousand pinpricks
when elation builds prematurely.
Quick to fold my emotions around that Beverly
Hills hello.

Will I ever find the final hand?
A grant over the line between teetering on an
oblivion of irrelevance.
Pink skies taunt me, soft rays sinking the edges,
melting itself far enough away to never let me
stay.
I wanted it all, the glamour, the champagne,
Platinum Triangle eyes know who I am.

Pink melting Beverly Hills falls out of sight.
Never away from attention.
Failure never falls out of mind.
It melts on a loop.
More tears.
More hope.
More desperate efforts,
faltered talent.
Dismissal in a flick of the wrist.
More tears.
Always melting
In Beverly Hills.

One Miami Morning

I'll never forget that moment, driving back to the hotel in Miami after breakfast, small in its measurement of time but vivid in a forever. The radio was turned down to a hum, radio stations neither of us knew. I didn't need music, sound; being with him filled the rattled places with ease and joy with him beside me.
I had fallen into a half-sleep as you drove down the sun-streaked highway. You thought I was in a deep slumber, lulled into closing my eyes from the warmth of the car and your contented presence.

You lifted one hand from the steering wheel, placed it gently on my thigh, brushing your thumb over my skin in the softest of affections. A moment so small it could be easily forgotten, lost to times eraser.
I couldn't forget it.

That feeling of quiet affection, swelling emotion traveled from mind to heart in a humble touch.

Forgetting the way, you felt that day is an impossibility. That bubble of just you and I, memory documented touches of us in the most piercingly clear seconds of my life.

I can see you when I close my eyes, feel it with the smile that meets the vividness of your hand reaching for me, a ghost brushing against my skin, until my heart pierces and I remember, your touch is just a specter now.
I'll never feel you in that way again.

I; Fear

I fear the worst.
You stand bold in its presence
fervent in your proclivities.
I beg of the night,
when minds have no presence
and hearts warn to stop,
Can he feel it too?

Tension tethered in an unwelcome distance
defeats my chest in wrecking rhythms.
I could drop a penny down a well
and no songbirds would rise.

It would be just as suitable if
I roped my heart to the pulley instead,
gave back the unbearable craving once implored,
to keep another's warmth.
Pin pricks of a fairytale gone numb
dance along my skin.

Drop the bucket with its boxed-up heart
tied shut by the flattening of promises
into a shadow that dresses no existence.

A place for souls on fire

swathed in a velvet darkness
never to let a heart
be withdrawn to the top once more.

Liz

Dreams at the end of a driveway.
Vegas lights glow with our laughter.
Cursed hotels bathed in pineapple dreams.
Tears only trusted to one another, silver drops in
a soulmate.
Colorado nights.
My daughters, your daughters.
Women wrapped in a reminiscence of childhood
memories,
passing friendship to their little women,
dreaming at the end of a driveway.

Something Peculiar

I want
I need
to move on
to be better,
to forgive myself.
Shake the loathing and be illimitable.
Everyone has something divine and individual
within.
Something peculiar and idiosyncratic.
So do you.

Electrified Ornament

Electricity in a moment ornaments skin.
A first meeting, a first glance, eyes locked
in a few sped fast breathes, eyes linger.
Unseen thoughts spindle among building energy.
Suffocating the room.
A welcome suffocation of pleasant surprise
of anticipation.
Electrification, as ephemeral as it is
refuses to leave the mind
a permanent dressing of winding thoughts
spinning and spinning
until
we meet again.

The Heart

I want to walk in the woods,
see something beautiful,
bolstering.

Let me lay in the grass beside you,
fingertips touching,
tracing shapes in the clouds.

I want to walk under the night sky
cloaked in snow falling.

White, crisp snow.

Snow that glimmers in moonlight.

I want to wake up with the ocean
folding its blue waters at my fingertips,
my toes
my edges
our sleeping bodies entranced by the waves,
skin warm bodies touch.

Dance with me in a mornings dew,
the wildflowers,

laugh wildly with you,

be endless with you.

I want to wander in the woods,
see something beautiful,
comforting.

To walk with you.

Bitter Confessional

I know what I need to say.

I do not question it.
I do not need to find validity,
search for unerring words,
the best way to loop them together.

You turned me with a passion
pressed thoughts to my lips
giving them to the places I beg
memory to keep.

I know what I need to say.

The letters thread in collusion
stitching truth into realization
imprinting them from my mind,
giving them to the out loud.

My body splits with fear,
a fissure of terror that I will lose you,
and yet-

If I were to open each door before me
with your smile behind it,

wake with you
sleep fluttering under beds cover
limbs contentedly entwined,
from now to till times last beat,
would never be enough.

If I lived in your endearments,
the brush of your fingertips sweeping over
my thigh
my arm
my cheek,
a wondrously infatuated gesture,
until I can feel no longer,
would never be enough.

To fall into your forever,
arms I cannot part from,
irises that know my every emotion
with a magic,
every morning
every night
every summer sunrise,
could never be enough.

One moment turns into a year, ten
breathing in the memories
you paint on my skin,
will not be enough.

Creating radiance in a story,
movie magic,
leading lady to leading man,
hands clasped in a forever
from now till the last Miami sunset,
is not enough.
Because,
I love you.

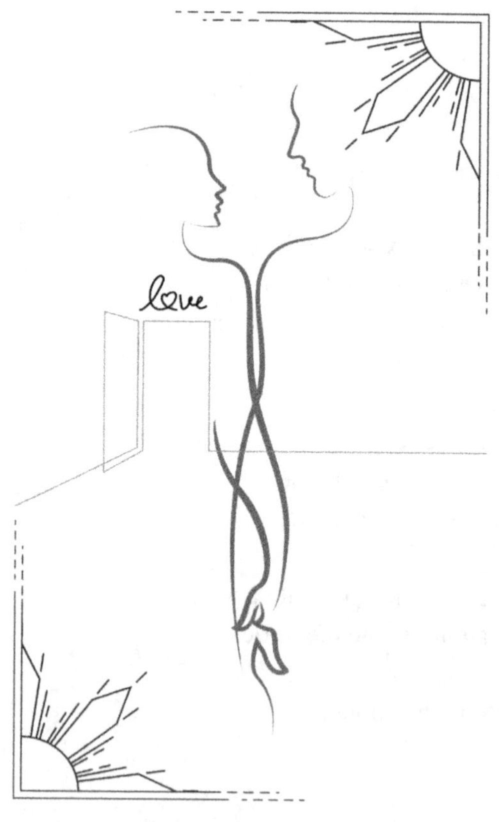

Next Question

What's a moment without a memory?
Forgotten.

How do we forget?
A lack of a beating heart for a moment.

Forgettable.

You are not forgettable.

What's a moment with memory?
A heart come alive.
A thumping of beats brightening what time
stores.

Existence with you
settles into the memorable places
like it has come home
arms full of indulgent recollections
tangible re-tellings conjured for a smile,
a comfort.

A memory with you illustrates happiness,
comfort animated with safety.

Next question
What is a memory without a home?

Anywhere without you.

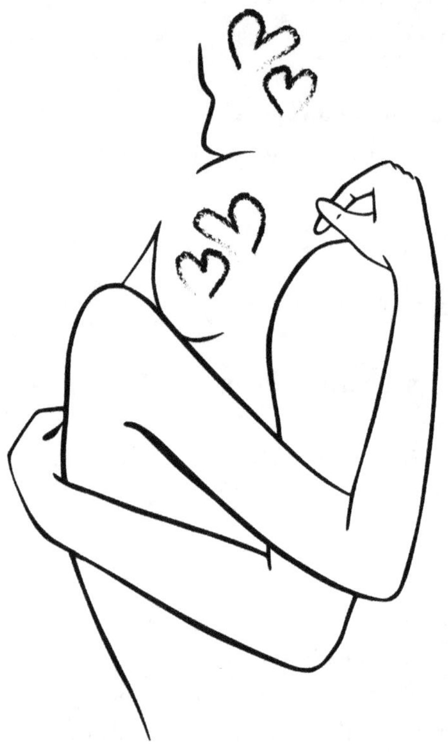